MAKERS GONNA LEARN
CRICUT HANDBOOK

CONTENTS

MAKERS GONNA LEARN

Written by Tanner Bell, Courtney Bell, Alisha Griffith, Lauren McCoy, Sadie Lewis, and Cynthia Gagen

INTRODUCTION

Hello Crafty Friends!

After extensive research and careful curation, we've crafted this resource to be your go-to guide for all things Cricut.

At Maker's Gonna Learn, our mission is to inspire, support, and empower you on your crafting journey. With this handbook, we aim to take the guesswork out of Cricut crafting, providing quick tips, easy to access settings, and quick tutorials to keep your projects running smoothly. Keep it handy to make your crafting experience more efficient, enjoyable, and creative every step of the way!

Section 1

TERMINOLOGY

 ## ATTACH

Hold your cuts in position so that images on the cutting mat will appear exactly as shown on the design screen

BLANK

An item used as the surface material on which you can place your design, including t-shirts, wood, mugs, hats, acrylic shapes, and more.

BLEED

Adds a bit of color beyond the edges of a design when making a Print then Cut to compensate in case machine cuts are a bit off

BURNISH

The act of pressing down and rubbing vinyl or HTV (often with the help of a tool) to ensure that it will stick well when weeding or applying the design

CALIBRATION

Available for the knife blade or with Print and Cut. Helps ensure that these work accurately and precisely.

COLD PEEL

Peeling the plastic backing off the iron-on vinyl 2-3 minutes after you have applied it to your material (allowing it to cool completely)

 ## COMBINE

A menu at the bottom of the layers panel that holds the reversible combinations: unite, subtract, intersect, and exclude. The weld and merge layers functions are also found here but are non-reversible.

 ## CONTOUR

Hide/show contour lines/cut paths around a layer

CRICUT DESIGN SPACE

Free design layout software Cricut users utilize to create projects.

 ## CUT

Set the layer to cut

DELETE

Remove selected item from the design screen

 ## DETACH

Separate attached layers so they can be moved independently and will cut or draw separately from all other layers

 ## DISTRIBUTE LETTERS TO LAYERS

Ungroup multi-layered text so that each layer group shows in the Layers panel as an image

 ## DUPLICATE

Copy and paste an image in one step

 ## EXCLUDE

Cuts and leaves everything except where the image overlaps

 ## FLATTEN

Merge all selected layers into a single layer; turns any image into a printable image

 GROUP/UNGROUP

Group multiple layers, images, or text together so they move and size together as one unit on the design screen. Ungroup will reverse it.

GLYPH

Fancy extra characters are available with some fonts. These can be found in Character Map on a Windows-based machine and in Font Book on a Mac.

HIDDEN LAYER

Indicates the layer is hidden from view on the design screen; click to unhide the layer (hidden layers will not cut, print, write, or score)

HOT PEEL

Peeling the plastic backing off the iron-on vinyl immediately after you have applied it to your material (often used when layering multiple designs)

 INTERSECT

Cuts and leaves only the parts of the shape that overlap.

E i ISOLATE LETTERS

Ungroup letters, placing each in an individual text box, enabling you to move them independently

KERNING

Refers to the spacing between letters in a word. Many script fonts are automatically kerned in Design Space, but you can also use the letter spacing function to kern them more.

KISS CUT

A cut that only goes through the top layer of the material without cutting through the backing.

VA LETTER SPACING

Adjust the spacing of each letter within a text box

A̲ A̲ LINE SPACING

Adjust the space between each line of text within a text box

MIRROR

Flips an image (so that it's shown in reverse). Used primarily for HTV projects.

 ## OFFSET

Creates a proportionally larger or smaller layer of your design. Add a shadow or decorative outline for dimension, and visual impact.

PNG (PORTABLE NETWORK GRAPHIC)

A type of image file commonly used for Print and Cut projects.

 ## PRINT

Turn a layer into a printable image (which can be printed on a regular printer, and then cut on the Cricut); use flatten to make your entire image print as one object

REGISTRATION MARKS

Marks added to Print and Cut designs to help Cricut machine know precisely where to cut.

REVERSE WEEDING

Used with intricate designs. With this technique, transfer tape is applied before weeding. The backing is removed and weeding is done from the back of the design.

 SCORE

Set the layer to score

 SLICE

Separate two overlapping layers into different parts

SMART MATERIALS

Cricut brand vinyl, iron-on vinyl, and adhesive-backed cardstock made specifically for use without a cutting mat. Available for use with Cricut Joy, Cricut Explore 3, and Cricut Maker 3.

STAR WHEELS

Small white rings on the roller bar of a Cricut machine. They hold materials in place while cutting. They may need to be moved all the way to the right when cutting certain thick materials such as chipboard

SUBLIMATION

A process that uses an image printed with sublimation ink on a sublimation printer. When applied to a blank using a heat press, the design is infused into the surface material (instead of sitting on top of it as vinyl would).

 ## SUBTRACT

Cuts the front shape out of the shape behind it & leaves a single layered image.

SVG (SCALABLE VECTOR GRAPHIC)

A type of vector image file used with die-cutting machines such as Cricut. It separates into multiple editable layers when uploaded. Also known as cut file.

 ## UNFLATTEN

Separate layers into individual printable layers

 UNGROUP

Ungroup a set of layers, images, or text so they move and size independently from one another on the design screen

 UNITE

Creates one unified shape, but the image layers do not combine. This allows you to go to the layers panel, select an individual image and then resize, rotate, and move your image if you need to. Once you click off of the image it is welded again.This function can be undone and is not permanent as opposed to weld.

 VISIBLE LAYER

Indicates the layer is visible on the design screen

WARM PEEL

Peeling the plastic backing off the iron-on soon after you have applied it to your material, while it is still warm (often used when layering multiple designs)

WEEDING

Process of removing negative space vinyl, leaving only the desired cut image on the liner.

 ## WELD

Join multiple layers together to create one shape

 ## WRITE

Set the layer to write

ZIP FILE

A folder of files that has been compressed to take up less space; files must be extracted from a zipped file before being uploaded into Design Space

Section 2

CRICUT TOOLS AND WHEN TO USE THEM

GREEN MAT (STANDARD GRIP)

The most often-used cutting mat. Use for: vinyl, heat transfer vinyl, cardstock, patterned paper, embossed cardstock

PURPLE MAT (STRONG GRIP)

Use for heavier materials like: Heavy cardstock, glitter cardstock, magnetic sheets, chipboard, poster board, fabric with stiffener

BLUE MAT (LIGHT GRIP)

Use for lighter weight materials like: thin cardstock, printer paper, vellum, construction paper.

PINK MAT (FABRIC GRIP)

Use for fabric and fabric-like materials like: fabric, bonded fabric, crepe paper.

WEEDING TOOL

A pointed tool used for weeding your design

TRANSFER TAPE

Adhesive tape used to transfer vinyl images onto project surfaces

BRAYER

A roller-type tool that works well for smoothing material on your mat and adhering designs to surfaces

SPATULA

A tool that is used to gently lift design pieces from the cutting mat.

EASYPRESS

A heat press used to heat and activate the adhesive on heat transfer vinyl.

SCRAPER/SQUEEGEE

A flat plastic tool that can be used to remove scraps from cutting mats and to burnish your designs when for weeding and applying to surfaces.

CRICUT TRUECONTROL KNIFE

A craft knife similar to an X-Acto knife.

EASYPRESS MAT

A mat to place items on when using an EasyPress. It helps reflect heat back up into the surface material for more even heating.

FINE POINT BLADE

The basic and generally most used Cricut blade. Used for cutting materials such as vinyl, HTV, cardstock, copy paper, and Smart Materials. Used in both the Explore and the Maker machines.

BONDED FABRIC BLADE

Used in the Explore machines for cutting bonded fabric.

ROTARY BLADE

Used in the Maker machines for cutting fabric, felt, and crepe paper.

DEEP POINT BLADE

Similar to the fine point blade, but used for cutting thicker materials such as magnetic sheets, foam sheets, and thick cardstock. Used in both the Explore and the Maker machines.

KNIFE BLADE

Designed for cutting the thickest materials. Used for cutting materials such as basswood, balsawood, heavy chipboard, and thick craft foam. Available only for Maker machines.

FOIL TRANSFER KIT

Used to add foil accents to your projects. Three tools in one, it comes with interchangeable fine, medium, and bold tips. One kit available for Explore and Maker machines. Separate kit available for Cricut Joy.

QUICKSWAP HOUSING

Allows you to quickly switch between various tools. Only for the Maker series.

SCORING STYLUS

Creates score/fold lines in paper materials for making greeting cards, 3D projects, and more. Can be used in either the Explore or Maker machines. Your machine can hold the stylus and a cutting blade at the same time, which means no swapping out tools.

SCORING WHEEL 01

Single scoring wheel. Uses the Quick Swap Housing.

SCORING WHEEL 02

Double scoring wheel. Uses the Quick Swap Housing.

ENGRAVING TIP

Allows you to engrave designs into metal, acrylic, leather, and more. Uses the Quick Swap Housing.

WAVY BLADE

Adds a wavy edge to your design. Great for decals and paper crafts. Uses the Quick Swap Housing.

DEBOSSING TIP

Creates detailed impressions similar to embossing. Uses the Quick Swap Housing.

PERFORATION BLADE

Makes even, perfectly spaced perforations in materials.Uses the Quick Swap Housing.

CRICUT JOY BLADE

Only for use with Cricut Joy machine. Used for cutting materials such as vinyl, iron-on vinyl, cardstock, poster board, Infusible Ink Transfer Sheets, and Smart Materials.

Section 3

DESIGN SPACE
FUNCTIONS

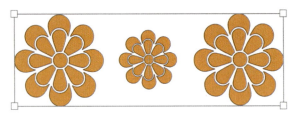

GROUP

Group multiple layers, images, or text together so they move and size together as one unit on the design screen.

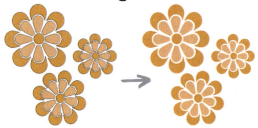

FLATTEN

Merge all selected layers into a single layer; turns any image into a Print and Cut image.

SLICE

Cut the shape on top out of the one behind it and separate it into different parts. Can only be done with 2 items selected.

24

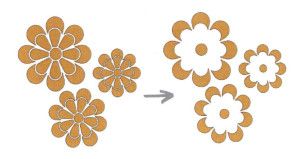

CONTOUR

Hide parts of the cut image to simplify it.

ATTACH

Hold your cuts together so they cut on the mat
exactly as they appear on the design screen

OFFSET

Creates a proportionally larger or smaller layer of
your design. Add a shadow or decorative outline
for dimension, and visual impact.

UNITE

Joins multiple layers together to create one shape like weld, but it's reversible at any time.

SUBTRACT

Cuts out the shape on top from the shape on the bottom.

INTERSECT

Produces a new shape of only the common space where the two selected shapes overlap.

EXCLUDE

Cuts out the overlapping area and excludes that piece from the overlapping design.

WELD

Join multiple layers together to create one shape. Connect letters to cut out in 1 piece.

ALIGN TOOL

Align text or images: Left, right, Top, Bottom, Center, Center Vertically or Horizontally

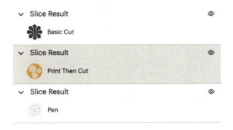

LAYERS PANEL

Displays the layers in your design. Shows the status of each layer.

MERGE LAYERS

Select sub-layers, click combine, and select merge layers from the drop-down menu to condense the layers. This is permanent.

RENAME LAYERS

Double-click with your mouse and type in whatever name we want to give that layer.

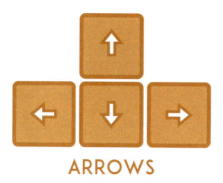

ARROWS

Move items around on the mat in small increments by using the arrow keys on your keyboard.

SHIFT KEY

Use the shift key on your keyboard to straighten items when rotating in Design Space

FAVORITE SETTINGS

"Favorite" most used settings for faster crafting, instead of searching through them all.

Create Sticker

Warp

Create Sticker ▾ Beta ✕

Design and create custom printable stickers

Die Cut
Cuts all the way through material to the exact design

Kiss Cut
Cuts through printable material only, leaving liner intact

CREATE STICKER

This allows you to quickly make stickers without having to add an offset and flatten your image. This is a Cricut Access feature; however this is something that can be done in Design Space for free.

MULTIPLE LAYERS

When uploading a design into Cricut Design Space, you now have the option to upload in multiple ways. You can unload it as a flat graphic, a single-layer graphic, or multiple layers. However, uploading a PNG as a multiple-layer graphic is only available to Cricut Access users.

Convert Upload To

Multiple Layers Beta

Creates up to 9 layers, separated by color

Single Layer

Creates a simple, one-color image or silhouette

Flat Graphic

Creates a single layer, full-color image (for Print Then Cut projects with a home printer)

Section 4

CRICUT CUT SETTINGS

CRICUT CUT SETTINGS

MATERIAL	BLADE	SETTING	MAT
ADHESIVE VINYL	FINE POINT	PREMIUM VINYL *OR SPECIALTY OPTION	STANDARD GRIP
IRON ON/HTV	FINE POINT	EVERYDAY IRON-ON	STANDARD GRIP
GLITTER VINYL	FINE POINT	GLITTER VINYL	STANDARD GRIP
GLITTER IRON ON/HTV	FINE POINT	GLITTER IRON-ON	STRONG GRIP
STICKER PAPER	FINE POINT	STICKER PAPER	LIGHT GRIP
CARDSTOCK	FINE POINT	MEDIUM OR HEAVY CARDSTOCK	STANDARD GRIP
PATTERNED PAPER	FINE POINT	LIGHT OR HEAVY PATTERNED PAPER	LIGHT GRIP
COPY PAPER	FINE POINT	COPY PAPER	LIGHT GRIP

MATERIAL	BLADE	SETTING	MAT
MAGNETIC MATERIAL	FINE POINT	PRINTABLE MAGNETIC SHEET	STRONG GRIP
SHRINKY DINKS	DEEP POINT	PLASTIC PACKAGING (2-3 PASSES)	STRONG GRIP
LEATHER	DEEP POINT / KNIFE	*SELECT THICKNESS	STRONG GRIP + TAPE
FAUX LEATHER (CRICUT OR 143 VINYL)	FINE POINT	PAPER THIN LEATHER	STRONG GRIP
FELT	ROTARY / FINE POINT	FELT	FABRIC GRIP
BONDED FELT	FINE POINT	FELT, BONDED	FABRIC GRIP
WOOL FELT	ROTARY	FELT, WOOL FABRIC	FABRIC GRIP
COTTON	ROTARY	COTTON	FABRIC GRIP

MATERIAL	BLADE	SETTING	MAT
BONDED COTTON	FINE POINT	COTTON, BONDED	FABRIC GRIP
CANVAS	ROTARY	CANVAS	FABRIC GRIP
TERRY CLOTH	ROTARY	TERRY CLOTH	FABRIC GRIP
WOOD VENEER	FINE POINT	NATURAL WOOD VENEER	STRONG GRIP
BASSWOOD	KNIFE	*SELECT THICKNESS	STRONG GRIP + TAPE
BALSA WOOD	KNIFE	*SELECT THICKNESS	STRONG GRIP + TAPE

CREATE CUSTOM CUT SETTINGS

If you notice that your machine is not cutting properly and you want to manipulate the cut settings, or add your own we are going to teach you exactly how to do this.

To add a new material, you will have to have something on your canvas, and then you will go to the 'Make it' screen.

From there, select 'Browse All Material' as seen in the image above. Once you have done that, you will need to scroll all the way to the bottom of the window that pops up where you will see an 'Add New Material' button.

Click this button and name the new material.

Once the new material has been named, Design Space will then put it in alphabetical order. This is where you will set your pressure, what blade to use, and how many passes you want the new cut setting to make. After that is completed, click save and the new material setting will be ready to use.

Section 5
EASY PRESS HEAT SETTINGS

	100% COTTON	COTTON POLY BLEND	100% POLYESTER	CANVAS
EVERYDAY IRON ON /REGULAR HTV	315°F 30s ≈ Med 25s	315°F 30s ≈ Med 25s	315°F 30s ≈ Med 25s	340°F 30s ≈ Med 25s
GLITTER/ HOLO / SPARKLE	330°F 30s ≈ Med 25s	330°F 30s ≈ Med 25s	330°F 30s ≈ Med 25s	330°F 30s ≈ Med 30s
EASYWEED ADHESIVE	300°F 15s ≈ Med 10s	300°F 15s ≈ Med 10s	300°F 15s ≈ Med 10s	300°F 15s ≈ Med 10s
PATTERNED IRON-ON	340°F 30s ≈ Med 25s	340°F 30s ≈ Med 25s	340°F 25s ≈ Med 15s	340°F 25s ≈ Med 15s
FOIL IRON ON / HTV	295°F 30s ~ Low 25s	295°F 30s ~ Low 25s	295°F 30s ≈ Med 25s	290°F 30s ~ Low 25s
SPORTFLEX / STRETCH HTV	not recommended	not recommended	305°F 30s ≈ Med 25s	not recommended
FUSIBLE FABRIC	280°F 5s ~ Low 5s	280°F 5s ~ Low 5s	280°F 5s ~ Low 5s	280°F 10s ~ Low 10s
BRICK HTV	325°F 20s ≈ Med 20s	325°F 20s ≈ Med 20s	325°F 20s ≈ Med 20s	325°F 20s ≈ Med 20s
FLOCK HTV	315°F 15s ≈ Med 15s	315°F 15s ≈ Med 15s	315°F 15s ≈ Med 15s	315°F 15s ≈ Med 15s

40

	LEATHER	FAUX LEATHER	SILK / SCREEN PRINT MATERIAL	BURLAP
EVERYDAY IRON ON / REGULAR HTV	270°F 30s ~ Low 20s	280°F 30s ~ Low 30s	280°F 20s ~ Low 15s	305°F 30s ≈ Med 30s
GLITTER/ HOLO / SPARKLE	330°F 30s ≈ Med 25s	270°F 20s ~ Low 30s	280°F 20s ~ Low 20s	305°F 30s ≈ Med 30s
EASYWEED ADHESIVE	310°F 10s ≈ Med 10s	270°F 5s ~ Low 5s	280°F 5s ~ Low 5s	310°F 15s ≈ Med 15s
PATTERNED IRON-ON	340°F 20s ≈ Med 15s	265°F 20s ~ Low 30s	280°F 20s ~ Low 15s	305°F 30s ≈ Med 30s
FOIL IRON ON / HTV	270°F 30s ~ Low 20s	255°F 30s ~ Low 30s	255°F 20s ~ Low 30s	305°F 30s ≈ Med 30s
SPORTFLEX / STRETCH HTV	not recommended	not recommended	not recommended	not recommended
FUSIBLE FABRIC	280°F 10s ~ Low 10s	280°F 8s ~ Low 8s	280°F 10s ~ Low 10s	280°F 10s ~ Low 10s
BRICK HTV	310°F 15s ≈ Med 15s	310°F 15s ≈ Med 15s	280°F 10s ~ Low 10s	310°F 20s ≈ Med 20s
FLOCK HTV	310°F 15s ≈ Med 15s	310°F 15s ≈ Med 15s	280°F 10s ~ Low 10s	310°F 15s ≈ Med 15s

	FELT	CORK	WOOD	CARDSTOCK
EVERYDAY IRON ON / REGULAR HTV	280°F 30s ~ Low 25s	315°F 15s ≈ Med 25s	300°F 40s ≈ Med 40s	280°F 30s ~ Low 25s
GLITTER/ HOLO / SPARKLE	270°F 30s ~ Low 30s	315°F 30s ≈ Med 25s	300°F 40s ≈ Med 40s	290°F 30s ~ Low 25s
EASYWEED ADHESIVE	270°F 15s ~ Low 15s	315°F 20s ≈ Med 20s	325°F 15s ≈ Med 15s	270°F 15s ~ Low 15s
PATTERNED IRON-ON	265°F 20s ~ Low 30s	315°F 15s ≈ Med 25s	305°F 30s ≈ Med 30s	290°F 30s ~ Low 25s
FOIL IRON ON / HTV	280°F 30s ~ Low 30s	280°F 30s ~ Low 30s	305°F 30s ≈ Med 30s	270°F 30s ~ Low 25s
SPORTFLEX / STRETCH HTV	not recommended	not recommended	not recommended	not recommended
FUSIBLE FABRIC	280°F 10s ~ Low 10s	280°F 5s ~ Low 5s	280°F 10s ~ Low 10s	280°F 5s ~ Low 5s
BRICK HTV	315°F 20s ≈ Med 20s	315°F 15s ≈ Med 15s	325°F 20s ≈ Med 20s	290°F 15s ~ Low 15s
FLOCK HTV	315°F 15s ≈ Med 15s	315°F 15s ≈ Med 15s	315°F 15s ≈ Med 15s	290°F 15s ~ Low 15s

	CHIPBOARD	ADHESIVE VINYL	METAL	ACRYLIC
EVERYDAY IRON ON / REGULAR HTV	315°F 30s ≈ Med 25s	255°F 5s ~ Low 5s	360°F 30s ≋ High 30s	310°F 20s ≈ Med 20s
GLITTER / HOLO / SPARKLE	315°F 30s ≈ Med 25s	255°F 5s ~ Low 8s	375°F 45s ≋ High 45s	360°F 30s ≋ High 20s
EASYWEED ADHESIVE	310°F 10s ≈ Med 10s	255°F 5s ~ Low 5s	320°F 15s ≈ Med 15s	320°F 15s ≈ Med 15s
PATTERNED IRON-ON	315°F 30s ≈ Med 25s	255°F 5s ~ Low 5s	360°F 30s ≋ High 30s	310°F 20s ≈ Med 20s
FOIL IRON ON / HTV	315°F 30s ≈ Med 25s	255°F 5s ~ Low 5s	360°F 30s ≋ High 30s	310°F 20s ≈ Med 20s
SPORTFLEX / STRETCH HTV	not recommended	not recommended	not recommended	not recommended
FUSIBLE FABRIC	280°F 10s ~ Low 10s	255°F 5s ~ Low 5s	280°F 10s ~ Low 10s	280°F 10s ~ Low 10s
BRICK HTV	315°F 15s ≈ Med 15s	not recommended	315°F 15s ≈ Med 15s	315°F 20s ≈ Med 20s
FLOCK HTV	315°F 15s ≈ Med 15s	255°F 5s ~ Low 5s	315°F 15s ≈ Med 15s	315°F 20s ≈ Med 20s

EVERYDAY IRON ON / REGULAR HTV

GLITTER/ HOLO / SPARKLE

EASYWEED ADHESIVE

PATTERNED IRON-ON

FOIL IRON ON / HTV

SPORTFLEX / STRETCH HTV

FUSIBLE FABRIC

BRICK HTV

FLOCK HTV

44

PUFF VINYL SETTINGS

BRAND	CUT SETTINGS	HEAT SETTINGS
Vinyl and Tulle Supply Regular	Everyday Iron On	280° degrees for 10 seconds (Hot Peel)
Siser Easy Puff HTV	Explore- Everyday Iron On (160) Maker - Premium Vinyl Holographic (185)	280° degrees for 15 seconds (Hot Peel)
Teckwrap Puff HTV	Everyday Iron On	285° degrees for 10 seconds, remove carrier sheet; Press again for 6 seconds (Cool Peel)
Starcraft 3D Puff	Everyday Iron On	285° degrees for 8-10 seconds (Warm Peel)
Vinyl and Tulle Supply Metallic	Everyday Iron On	285° degrees for 10 seconds, Cold peel, remove carrier sheet; cover with teflon and Press again for 8 seconds

Puff is always best when pressed with a heat press. Puff Vinyl MUST HAVE HEAVY and EVEN pressure!

**always cut with the carrier sheet facing DOWN & press with the carrier sheet UP

Section 6

MATERIAL QUICK GUIDES

ADHESIVE VINYL

is a vinyl that has adhesive on the back of it. When you remove the liner, it will stick to surfaces like wood, glass, metal, and plastic.

CUTTING:

- Place vinyl, right side up, onto cutting mat.
- Upload your cut file in Cricut Design Space, add to your canvas, and size as needed.
- Load your mat into your machine.
- Press Make It. Select your materials (search for the exact adhesive vinyl you're using).
- Cut out your design.

PREPARATION:

- Weed the negative vinyl away from your cut image.
- Cut a piece of transfer tape to fit your image. Peel off the liner and place the transfer tape sticky side down over your cut design.
- Start in the center and work your way out, using a burnishing tool.
- Peel up the liner on the back of the vinyl design at
- a 45-degree angle.

APPLICATION:

- Clean your project surface.
- Place your design onto the surface, adhesive side down.
- Burnish your design so that it adheres well to the surface.
- Peel away the transfer tape at a 45-degree angle.

IRON-ON VINYL

Also known as HTV or Heat Transfer Vinyl. It requires the use of heat to activate the adhesive on it so you can apply it to fabric-like surfaces and wood.

CUTTING:

- Place vinyl, shiny side down, onto cutting mat.
- Upload your cut file in Cricut Design Space, add to your canvas, and size as needed.
- Load your mat into your machine.
- Press Make It. Select the type of Iron-On you're using.
- Be sure to mirror your design. This is very important when using iron-on vinyl!
- Cut out your design.

PREPARATION:

- Weed the negative vinyl away from your cut image.
- Remember, heat transfer vinyl has built-in transfer tape.
- Peel up the liner on the back of the vinyl design at a 45-degree angle.

APPLICATION:

- Clean your project surface. Use a lint roller for fabric projects.
- Place your design onto the surface, adhesive side down.
- Heat with your Cricut EasyPress or other heating tool, following the settings given by the manufacturer or in our EasyPress Heat Settings Chart.
- When you see bubbles forming, this indicates that the transfer tape is releasing from the design.
- Peel away the transfer tape at a 45-degree angle.

A technique where you print out a design from Design Space on your printer and cut out the design using your Cricut with the help of sensor lines/ registration marks.

You can use a printable file already designed to use with Print then Cut or you can take any SVG and turn it into a Print then Cut by flattening it.

The maximum size design Cricut allows is 6.75 by 9.25 inches. The largest material size you can use is 8.5 by 11 inches.

HOW TO:

- Open your design in Design Space and size it. If you're using a PNG, it is already good to go, but if you're using an SVG, you'll need to select it and choose Flatten to turn it into a Print and Cut.
- Print your design using your printer.
- Place your printed design on a cutting mat and load it into your Cricut machine for cutting.

**Print and Cut is not available for the Cricut Joy, but can be done on the Cricut Joy Xtra.

You can cut paper and cardstock with the Cricut Joy, Explore, and Maker machines.

If you are creating a design with intricate cuts, note that there is a specific Cardstock - Intricate Cut setting under Materials.

For most paper and cardstock projects, you will be using the Fine Point Blade. With thicker ones, you will want to use the Deep Point Blade.

A LightGrip mat or a StandardGrip mat that is a bit older and not as sticky is recommended. For heavy cardstock, you might need the stronger grip of the StandardGrip mat.

When removing paper and cardstock from your mat, you want to flip the mat over and gently curl and peel it away from the cardstock to avoid curling of the material. Smaller pieces can be lifted up with the spatula tool.

TROUBLESHOOTING

Having some problems with your Cricut projects? Here are a few tips and tricks we wanted to share with you.

Your cuts are not lining up with Print Then Cut.
First thing you will need to do is calibrate. You can find this in Design Space by clicking the down arrow next to your name in the top right corner and click settings. You will then go to the machine tab and follow the prompts for calibration.

Your machine isn't reading registration marks.
Try turning the lights down. Sometimes when lighting is too bright or inconsistent it will hinder the sensor picking up the registration marks, especially with shiny paper. if your registration marks are not dark enough, go over them with a black marker.

Your blade is not cutting your material.
Take the housing out and check to make sure that there is no debris around the blade and clean it if there is. If it is still not cutting, replace the blade.

You are experiencing a flashing red button.
There are a couple of things that you will need to do if you are seeing a flashing red Cricut button.
1. Make sure that there are no materials stuck or jammed in your machine.
2. Cycle your machine. You may have to turn your machine off and back on.
3. If the button is staying red, try updating the firmware.
4. If none of the above suggestions work, call Cricut CS team at 1-877-7Cricut.

EXCLUSIVE OFFER JUST FOR YOU!

Maker University is designed to guide you through your journey from a novice crafter to a full-on CRICUT wizard! This is the program for anyone wanting to build confidence with their skill, plus shave off countless hours of trial and error, not to mention keeping your sanity. We will lay the foundation for your Cricut education needed to take things to the next level. For Black Friday this year, we have created a bundle including Freshman and Sophmore years and at an insane price- it's never been this low and never will be again!

GET THE COURSE NOW

https://makersgonnalearn.com/university-offer